Looking Bac

Whickham

FRONT St. WHICKHAM.

**Compiled and edited
by Bill Saunders and Richard Pears
on behalf of Whickham Local History Society**

Sunniside Front Street, c. 1900. (Gateshead Libraries)

Previous page: Whickham Front Street, c. 1900. (Beamish the Living Museum of the North)

Front cover: The Knowles, Whickham, c. 1920. (Beamish the Living Museum of the North)

Back cover: Swalwell Bank Top, c. 1900 (Beamish the Living Museum of the North), Gibside Column (Bill Saunders), Children in Rose Villa Lane, Whickham (Gateshead Libraries) and Swalwell Hoppings (Gateshead Libraries).

Also available from Summerhill Books

Gateshead Remembered

Saltwell Park – The Story of the People's Park

The Old Pubs of Gateshead

The Clubs of Gateshead

or visit our website to view our full range of books:
www.summerhillbooks.co.uk

Copyright Whickham Local History Society 2016

First published in 2016

Summerhill Books
PO Box 1210, Newcastle upon Tyne NE99 4AH

www.summerhillbooks.co.uk

email: summerhillbooks@yahoo.co.uk

ISBN: 978-1-911385-03-5

Contents

Sunniside Methodist Church Soup Kitchen during 1926 General Strike.
(Gateshead Libraries)

Acknowledgements

We would like to thank Julian Harrop of Beamish Museum Collections and Maggie Thacker of Gateshead Libraries for their assistance in obtaining many of the archive photographs in this book. Please visit www.gatesheadlocalstudies.gov.uk to view and purchase these and other images from Gateshead Central Library. For Beamish Museum Collections please visit http://collections.beamish.org.uk

Thanks to everyone who contributed to this books, including Ethel Armstrong, John Mitchell, Pam Neville, Wendy Oloman, Jim Ord, Helen Page, Richard Pears, Thelma Rix, Bill Saunders and Lillian Unsworth. Special thanks to our publisher Andrew Clark for his advice and attention to producing this book.

Extracts from Ordnance Survey maps published 50 years prior to April 2015 are reproduced here in accordance with authorising statement at www.ordnancesurvey.co.uk/business-and-government/licensing/crown-copyright.html and confirmed by email to Richard Pears on 7th March 2016.

Whickham Local History Society

Whickham and District Local History Society first met in November 1975 at Whickham Library. The Society meets in the Community Centre, Front Street, Whickham, on the fourth Monday of the month from September to May. Each meeting has a speaker on a topic of historical or local interest. There are summer excursions to places of interest; recent visits have included Newby Hall (Ripon), Howick Hall gardens, Binchester Roman Fort and Auckland Castle, Capheaton Hall and Littleharle Tower, Eggleston Hall and the Bowes Museum, and guided walks in Newcastle, Winlaton Mill and Ryton. New members are always welcome.

Above: Whickham and District Local History Society visit to Path Head Water Mill.

Left: History Society members on a visit to Durham.

Introduction

How and why did this publication come about? Well, it all began when we, the Whickham Local History Society, were awarded the honour of hosting the 'Round the County Day' for 2016 by the Association of Northumberland Local History Societies (ANLHS). The Whickham Local History Society was formed in November of 1975 so when we applied to the ANLHS for the 'Round the Counties Day' event we stated that this year was our fortieth anniversary, their response was to say that it was also the fiftieth year of the ANLHS. Our first thoughts were, 'Panic!' Then after much thought and discussion we started to formulate some ideas. During the aforementioned discussion it was suggested that it would

Margaret Dryburgh (1890-1945), Swalwell teacher and missionary in China and Singapore. (David Newton)

be a nice idea to send our guests away at the end of the day with an information pack about Whickham. The information pack, envisaged could possibly include a resume of some of the subjects covered by the speakers and guides on the day, but also other information about Whickham that we could not include in the time allowed. It was also hoped that it may encourage our guests and others who read this publication to return or visit Whickham at a later date to take a closer look at the wealth of history and heritage we have on our doorstep. Then it became obvious, instead of an 'information pack' we replace it with a book. So that is the how and why this book came into being.

There have been a number of publications about Whickham History over the years, therefore, we have attempted, in this instance, to include information that has not been covered previously or has had scant coverage for one reason or another.

Hopefully our event will be in keeping with the traditions of the Association and will be enjoyed and remembered by all those who join us on the day but most importantly our attempt at producing a book of this nature will be enjoyed by readers from far and near.

Bill Saunders,
Chairman of the Whickham Local History Society

Marley Hill Silver Band. (Gateshead Libraries)

A Brief History of Whickham and District
by Richard Pears

The historical parish of Whickham covered a much larger area than the present town, as it included Swalwell, Dunston, part of the Team Valley, Lobley Hill, Sunniside, Marley Hill, Gibside and Byermoor. Its boundaries were the River Tyne to the north, the River Derwent to the west, the River Team to the east and the Black Burn to the south. Bronze Age artefacts have been found and Iron Age roundhouses have been located by aerial photographs at Washingwells, south east of Whickham village. In 1970, aerial photography revealed the crop marks of Roman forts at Washingwells. The forts are on private land and have not been excavated, but they may belong to an early Roman frontier which preceded Hadrian's Wall (built c. 130 AD), or more likely they were practice fortifications or marching camps built by Roman units heading north.

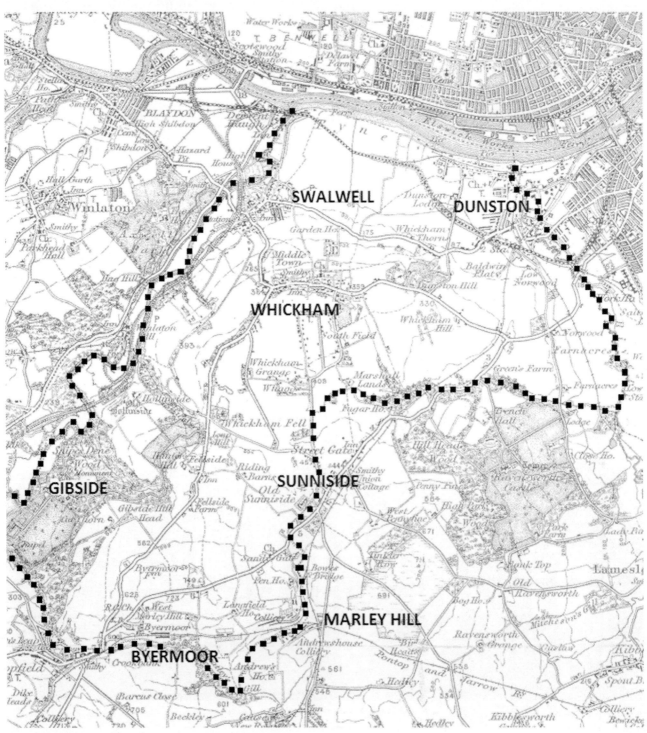

Whickham Parish in 1856. (Ordnance Survey)

The name Whickham or 'Quykham' as first recorded, is Anglo-Saxon, meaning 'estate with a quickset hedge', suggesting that the village on top of its steep hill was surrounded by a hawthorn hedge, a very effective deterrent to human and animal predators. In the Boldon Book, compiled for the Bishop of Durham in 1183, the Bishop had 35 tenants in Quykham, each of whom held an ox gang of land (about 15 acres). In return, the tenants paid 16d rent and were obliged to work for the Bishop three days per week; carry his baggage between Durham and Bedlington when required; serve in his fishery in the Tyne; and provide a cow, a hen and 10 eggs and pay 9s cornage rent. Among other annual dues owed to the bishop of Durham, the Boldon Buke of 1186 stipulated that the inhabitants of Whickham had to build a house 40 feet by 15 feet each year.

A medieval house reconstructed at the Ryedale Folk Museum, Yorkshire. (Richard Pears)

Medieval Whickham as a small agricultural community, clustered around a green, with two rows of houses. The northern row, on the edge of the slope down to Swalwell, extended along the line of Church Chare, with the Rectory and Church of St Mary the Virgin in the middle, and along School Lane, with outlying houses around the sites of Whickham Park and Dockendale Hall. The southern row of houses probably stood on the rising ground now occupied by Chase Park. Until 1960, Chase Hall, a private house, stood here, and the southern row of houses disappeared beneath the gardens of this estate.

Between the northern and southern rows was the village green. Today, only a tiny remnant remains, itself saved from development in 1852 by the prompt action of the Rector, Revd H.B. Carr. The green would have been much more extensive, stretching from the Cross (where Lang Jack's statue is located) on the west to the bottom of Broom Lane on the east. Here the villagers kept their livestock during the night, protected from predators and raiders. Fields surrounded the village. At the west end of the medieval village, south of the road, was the Glebe, now the site of Whickham Health Centre and the Glebe Sports fields, a substantial area of land belonging to the Rector of Whickham. Many of the houses would have been close to the church, other families living in Swalwell and Dunston close to the Rivers Tyne, Derwent and Team where there were fisheries and mills. The Bishop of Durham owned a mill where the villagers had their grain ground into flour. Some families lived by the River Tyne at Swalwell and Dunston where there were mills and salmon fisheries. The windmill in Chase Park was built in 1720.

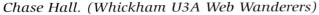

Chase Hall. (Whickham U3A Web Wanderers)

Windmill in Chase Park. (Richard Pears)

The oldest building in Whickham is the parish church of St Mary the Virgin. The earliest parts are Norman, including the chancel arch. The west tower and the south aisle date from the 14th century. Much of the north side of the church was rebuilt in 1860-62, following a serious fire in November 1841. Like many mining areas, Whickham had a strong Methodist tradition following John Wesley's visits to Whickham and Swalwell, and several chapels were built. During the Reformation, Catholicism in Whickham was all but extinguished and it was 1948 before a Catholic church was built in Whickham.

Following the Norman Conquest there were rebellions in County Durham against the new rulers. William the Conqueror responded by destroying villages, livestock and crops, and it is likely that the people of Whickham were affected by these upheavals. Like many northern communities, the people of Whickham suffered the deprivations and uncertainties of the Anglo-Scottish wars. Though the English were usually successful in battle, little could be done to prevent Scottish raiders plunging deep into northern England. Following his victory at Bannockburn in 1314, King Robert the Bruce of Scotland destroyed villages across Northumberland and Durham. English armies heading towards Scotland often passed through Whickham, travelling down Clockburn Lane to ford the River Derwent and then on to the ford over the River Tyne at Newburn, west of Newcastle. Scottish armies could travel in the opposite direction. In 1346, King David II of Scotland invaded England and crossed the River Tyne at Newburn, almost certainly passing through Whickham parish on his way south. His army was eventually defeated at the Battle of Neville's Cross near Durham, but not before destroying several villages.

Parish Church of St Mary the Virgin, Whickham. (Richard Pears)

The two oldest buildings in Whickham parish show evidence of defence against Scottish raiders. The tower of the parish church was defensible. The ground floor is covered by a stone-vaulted roof, a means to fireproof the tower and turn it into a refuge during Scottish raids. The door above this vault was originally the only entrance to the upper parts of the tower, another feature enhancing its security. There are extensive views from the roof of the tower, to east and west along the valley and northwards into Northumberland. If a warning beacon was placed upon this tower, it would be visible to friendly forces for miles around. On the south-west outskirts of Whickham, near Clockburn Lane, stands Old Hollinside, a fortified manor house built in the fourteenth century. Now an attractive ruin, it retains the defensive features that were essential in Northern houses in troubled times, such as drawbar slots and small windows on the lower floors. At Hollinside the entrance is between two projecting wings, the space between arched over to carry a defensive turret. Although it could not resist a Scottish army, raiders might think twice if, as the earthworks shown on the 1856 Ordnance Survey map suggest, Hollinside once had a curtain wall and gatehouse. The house stands on the edge of a steep hill overlooking the River Derwent. The form and siting of Old Hollinside recalls that of Aydon Castle near Corbridge. During the English Civil War, Parliament's Scottish allies defeated the King's army at the Battle of Newburn ford in 1640. The King's soldiers had camped in the fields below Whickham

Old Hollinside. (Richard Pears)

and as they fled they set fire to their tents, igniting a seam of coal which burned for many years after. Oliver Cromwell is said to have stayed in Dockendale Hall. Whickham played its part in the two World Wars. The 'valiant hearts' who gave their lives for our freedom are commemorated on the War Memorials in Whickham, Dunston, Swalwell and with individual monuments. The most recent name is that of Sapper David Watson of Whickham (1986-2009), killed in Afghanistan.

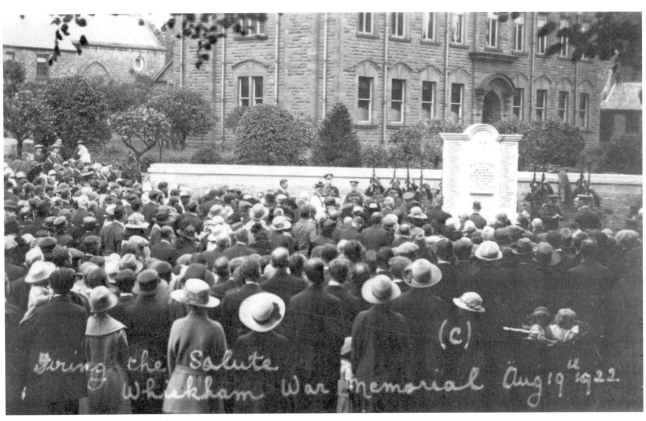

During the Salute Whickham War Memorial Aug 19th 1922.

Above: Unveiling of Whickham War Memorial. (Beamish the Living Museum of the North)

Left: David Watson commemorated on Whickham War Memorial. (Richard Pears)

During the First World War, part of the Rectory of 1713 was used to assemble shells. It served a more peaceful purpose after 1922 when it became the War Memorial Cottage Hospital and after use as a school it is now a health centre. During the First World War, soldiers camped at Gibside Hall, south of Whickham, and during the Second World War troops were billeted at Ravensworth Castle. Anti-aircraft guns were positioned around Whickham to protect the shipyards and munitions factories at Elswick. A bombing decoy was located on the Gibside estate. A little known reminder of the anti-invasion preparations from the Second World War can be seen around the allotments at Watergate, where rifle slits were cut into the wall to cover the farmland on the eastern side of the village.

At Dunston there is a machine-gun pillbox positioned against the railway embankment near the former Federation Brewery. It faces west, and a similar pillbox stood where IKEA is

Dunston pillbox. (Richard Pears)

9

now. They were intended to protect Dunston power station and the shipyards at Elswick from German paratroops.

Until recently, air raid shelters built for factory workers survived at First Avenue on the Team Valley and several examples of Anderson shelters supplied for family protection remain throughout the area.

Air raid shelters and 1930s factories at Team Valley Trading Estate – now demolished. (Richard Pears)

Agriculture was an important part of Whickham history, but has often been overshadowed by the coal industry. The prehistoric inhabitants of Whickham were attracted by the agricultural potential of the lands above the River Tyne. It is no coincidence that their remains were discovered in the vicinity of the modern Washingwell and Marshall Lands farms, since the same land was as valuable to farmers in prehistory as it is today. The medieval bishops of Durham granted lands to their supporters, including the estates of Fugar, Hollinside and Gibside which began as farmsteads on the periphery of Whickham parish. Many farmhouses survive around the district, and until the mid-twentieth century there were three farms on Front Street and Whickham Highway (Glebe Farm, Cross Farm

Dunston West Farm. (Richard Pears)

and Dunston West Farm). Farmland continues to provide the green belt around Whickham and preserve the air of seclusion one feels travelling along Whickham Highway, Sunniside Road and Fellside Road.

One by-product of agriculture was brewing, and John Barras began brewing beer in his house Whickham Lodge in the 1740s; his son, John Jnr, moved production to Gateshead in 1770. John and Matthew Taylor opened a brewery in Swalwell in 1765, though Matthew lived in Whickham in a fine mansion he called the Hermitage.

Swalwell Brewery in 1863. (Beamish the Living Museum of the North)

In 1356 the Bishop of Durham granted a lease of the coal mines in the Manor of Whickham, the first documentary evidence of the industry which was to dominate Whickham parish until the mid-twentieth century. Coal was available close to the surface and it was used locally as a domestic fuel for centuries. From the fourteenth century its use became more widespread, to heat limestone to create lime for improving the productivity of fields and to replace charcoal in metalworking. When the surface coal was exhausted, miners dug deeper and deeper pits to reach the 'black gold'. The terrible human costs of mining are evident from the grim regularity of 'killed in a pit' in the Parish Registers of Whickham. In the sixteenth century, national demand led to wealthy merchants from Newcastle buying up the lands around Whickham to maximise production, to the consternation of villagers whose lands, crops and roads were ruined by the stream of wagons carrying the coal down to ships waiting in the Tyne.

Above: Axwell Park Colliery. (Beamish the Living Museum of the North)

Left: Marley Hill Colliery closure. (Jack Medcalf collection, copyright Whickham LHS)

It has been estimated that Whickham mines supplied 17,000 tons of coal per year in the 1520s. In the 1590s the estimated figure was 40,000 tons, by 1636 nearly 90,000 tons. By the beginning of the eighteenth century more productive pits were located outside the parish, but mining continued. In 1900 there were collieries at Dunston, Swalwell Colliery and Axwell Park Colliery, and a colliery at Marley Hill. Watergate Colliery opened in 1924 and closed in 1964.

The site of Watergate Colliery has been reclaimed as a public park, but the housing estate built for the miners on Broom Lane survives. The last coal mine operating in Whickham area, Marley Hill Colliery, closed in 1983, bringing an end to six centuries of mining.

The huge amounts of coal produced in Whickham were more than the primitive roads could cope with; a more reliable transport system was required. A law suit in 1622 is evidence for the first Tyneside wagonway (a wooden railway upon which the coal wains could be drawn by horses to the river). Wagonways were expensive to build and maintain, but eased the transport problem for the coal-owners. Some routes of these wagonways can be seen around the outskirts of Whickham and the Causey Arch, three miles south of Whickham, is the world's oldest railway bridge, built in 1727. The Tanfield railway ran through fields on the eastern side of Whickham.

The wagonways converged at the River Tyne, where staithes extended into the river so that coal could be loaded into keels and carried downriver to Newcastle and thence for export.

Coal wagon. (Bill Saunders)

One reminder of the coal trade in Whickham parish is Dunston Staithes, a huge wooden structure built in 1893 so that larger sea-going ships could be loaded directly.

Coal provided a ready source of power for many other industries in the Whickham area, particularly in Dunston and Swalwell where there were also railway stations.

There were cokeworks at Marley Hill, Norwood (near Dunston) and Derwenthaugh (near Swalwell); gasworks at Redheugh near Dunston; Dunston Engine Works and the Atlas River Works; brickworks at the Teams, Clockmill (Dunston) and Swalwell; and a steel works, forges and paper mills (on the site of Ambrose Crowley's eighteenth century ironworks) at Swalwell.

The Staithes, Dunston-on-Tyne.

Ships loading coal at Dunston Staithes. (Beamish the Living Museum of the North)

RAILWAY STATION, SWALWELL. 1440.

Above: Swalwell Station. The passenger bridge was installed at the town station in Beamish Museum. (Gateshead Libraries)

Left: Marley Hill Cokeworks. (Gateshead Libraries)

The Co-operative Wholesale Society opened a flour works at Dunston in the 1880s and a soap works in 1909.

All of this industry polluted the River Tyne and ended the first industry recorded at Dunston in medieval registers: salmon fishing.

Above: Making soap at Dunston CWS works. (Beamish the Living Museum of the North)

Right: The CWS fire brigade at Dunston CWS flour mills. Fire and explosion were real dangers in flour mills due to the flour dust in the air. (Gateshead Libraries)

Dunston Power station, now the site of the MetroCentre. (Gateshead Libraries)

A power station was built at Dunston in 1910 and replaced by a much larger one in 1933. The power station was demolished in 1986 and the MetroCentre built on the site.

The earliest houses in Whickham village today date from the seventeenth century onwards. During the eighteenth century much of the centre of the village was enclosed in private estates for wealthy families, whilst landed families used the money raised from coal mining to build grand mansions, including Dunston Hill House, Axwell Hall, Gibside and Ravensworth Castle.

These survive in varying states of disrepair: Gibside, the Bowes family mansion, is now owned by the National Trust. It stands roofless, surrounded by landscaped grounds and near the beautiful Chapel they built as their mausoleum.

Dunston Hill House, home of the Carr-Ellisons, was used as a hospital until recent years and is now apartments. Axwell Hall, home of the Claverings, is being converted into apartments. Ravensworth Castle, home of the Liddells, was demolished in the 1950s because of subsidence from the very mines that had paid for its reconstruction, leaving only two surviving towers from the medieval castle.

Whickham became an urban district council in 1894 and a new town hall (now the Harry Clasper pub) was built

Gibside Hall and Chapel. (W. Bourn, Whickham Parish, 1893)

on Front Street in 1904. Whickham remained a small village until after the Second World War, whilst nineteenth century Dunston and Swalwell became densely populated with terraces of Tyneside flats to accommodate industrial families.

Terraces for mining families were built at the west end of Whickham village at the end of the nineteenth century, close to the access shaft for Axwell Colliery, and a new estate of houses for miners at Watergate Colliery from 1924 on Broom Lane.

Council houses were constructed on Broom Lane in the 1920s (including a Lenin Drive and Marx Crescent) and on Rectory Lane. Houses were built on the fields at the bottom of Dunston Bank and at Lobley Hill from the 1920s, and in Sunniside around Kingsway from the 1930s. From the 1950s large housing estates were built around Whickham village centre. In 1971 the Urban District Council championed modern architecture with the ill-fated Dunston Rocket, and the St Mary's Green shopping centre that replaced many of the traditional houses and shops on the Front Street.

Dunston shops. Trams ran through Dunston and Swalwell as these were on lower ground than Whickham village. (Beamish the Living Museum of the North)

More housing estates appeared in the 1970s and 1980s, and today the Whickham area has become a popular residence for many families working on Tyneside. The shops in the villages have suffered as a result of the opening of the MetroCentre in Dunston in 1986, but this development also provides many jobs for people in the Whickham area. Today there are many organisations that reflect the vibrant Whickham community,

Park Terrace, Swalwell, receiving a delivery from Reeds butchers of Blaydon. (Gateshead Libraries)

including football, cricket and golf clubs, theatre, gardeners, WEA, U3A, Scouts and Guides. Whickham and District have produced several notable characters, including the composer William Shield (1748-1829, born in Swalwell), the artist Charlton Nesbit (1775-1838, from Swalwell), the renowned oarsman Harry Clasper (1812-1870, from Dunston), and the footballer Paul Gascoigne (from Dunston, born 1967). Lord Armstrong was schooled in

Whickham, whilst the missionary Margaret Dryburgh (1890-1945) taught at Swalwell School and worked with her father, the minister at the Ebenezer Chapel in Swalwell.

Left: Watergate houses. (Richard Pears)

Whickham Front Street houses, demolished in 1970s for St Mary's Green shopping centre. (Jack Medcalf collection, copyright Whickham LHS)

Albert Thomson
Local Artist and Historian
by Bill Saunders

For those of us who are interested in local history, particularly those in the Whickham area, the name of Albert Thomson is not one that would readily come to mind. All towns and villages have their hidden seekers of local knowledge who gather information, then pass away and their efforts go with them. With this article I hope to make sure that the name of Albert Thomson is one that is not forgotten and that his work is appreciated and enjoyed by future generations interested in our local history. Albert S. Thomson was not just a writer, but a highly talented and prolific artist, who, through the medium of pen and ink has left us many images of Whickham and the surrounding area. It is interesting that many of the drawings he produced are not all executed in the time that he saw them, but many are his impressions of those same scenes from about 1900 and earlier.

Albert Thomson was not a local man: he was born in Glasgow in 1890 and as a young boy his drawing skills were criticized by his art teacher on a number of occasions, but this did not deter him and his sketch pad became his constant companion throughout his life. His working life however was far from the world of art and much dictated by the events of the time.

He became a sea-going marine engineer at a time when his knowledge and expertise was put to use in the defence of the realm on destroyers and submarines during the First World War. Whilst serving aboard one of HM submarines they came under attack from a German vessel which resulted in the

Albert Thomson (left) checking the proofs of his work.

submarine being sunk. Albert Thomson amazingly survived despite being seriously injured, he suffered by losing much of his skin in the blast and then spent a considerable time drifting in the sea before being rescue which led to a period in hospital. He was certainly a man who flirted with danger because his next employment was as a deep-sea diver, during which period he was involved in another accident. On one dive he was shot to the surface too quickly causing decompression sickness which could be fatal but fortunately for him his backup team immediately lowered him to the depths again a raised him gradually thus saving his life. After the war in the 1920s he was employed as chief engineer for a short period at a power station in Dundee. The 1930s led to what sounds like the perfect job as chief engineer aboard a millionaire's yacht. The 'Arla' which had previously been owned by the Kaiser Wilhelm II, gave Albert Thompson the opportunity to travel the world in style. The 'Arla' was later commandeered during the Second War, scuppered and used as a harbour block-ship. This was followed by another shore based position as Foreman Inspector for the shipping company Harland and Wolfe at their Glasgow Yard. He continued in this roll until his retirement, aged 65 in 1955.

His daughter and her family moved to Whickham in June of 1955 and later in that same year he moved to Whickham to be closer to them. He was known to his family as Bertie and no doubt by the new friends he made in the area. He was heard to make the statement 'I fell in love with Whickham at first sight'. He immediately threw himself into investigating the history of the area and as he often walked miles around Whickham and surrounding areas with new found friends he sketched local scenes at every opportunity. I have observed that quite often newcomers to an area become the most enthusiastic researchers of their new environ as was the case with Albert Thomson. One of his other hobbies at this time was model making, not surprisingly models of ships were his favourite subject. However, his interest in local history obviously took much of his time and his research and his artwork was put to good use.

The 'Focus' magazine first appeared in May of 1966 and was published as the 'Bi-monthly Journal of Whickham Urban District Council'. In the first edition two of his sketches, 'The Top of the Swalwell Bank c. 1900' and 'Front Street c. 1920', were used to illustrate 'The Annals of the History of Whickham' by William Bourn. The 'Annals' were serialized in 16 parts and in all except number 16 we find drawings by Albert Thomson. He also illustrated 'The Swalwell Story' by William Bourn, again serialized in seven parts with nine drawings by Thomson. His sketches were used to illustrate the work of a number of other writer's work in the 'Focus', such as D. Lumley's six transcriptions of local interest.

In July 1968 (volume 3 number 2) the frontispiece of the 'Focus magazine' was his drawing of the Hermitage Pagoda c. 1900 to illustrate the article he wrote entitled 'Whickham's Willow Pattern' which is a short history of the Hermitage and its garden. This was the first of his many written contributions to the magazine. He covered 13 subjects in total, as can be seen in the list below, but as a number of these were serialized his articles appeared in no less than 26 issues.

'Focus' magazine covers by Albert Thomson showing local scenes.

Albert Thompson articles

Whickham's 'Willow Pattern' – 'Focus' Vol 3.2

The Countess of Strathmore – 'Focus' Vol 3.5

The Parish Church of St Mary the Virgin – 'Focus' Vol 4.3 & 4.4 (two parts)

Postal Service at Whickham – 'Focus' Vol 5.1

The House that Jack Built – 'Focus' Vol 5.2

William Bourn, Historian 1848-1926 – 'Focus' Vol 5.3

The Dunston Documentary – 'Focus' Vol 5.2 to 6.2 (seven parts)

The Whickham Village Pump – 'Focus' Vol 5.4

The Keelmen of the Tyne – 'Focus' Vol 6.3 to 6.5 (three parts)

The Forges of Swalwell – 'Focus' Vol 6.5

The Immortal Clasper – 'Focus' Vol 6.6, 7.1 & 7.2 (three parts)

Influence of the Church on Medieval Village Life – 'Focus' Vol 7.4, 7.4 & 7.6 (three parts)

Friarside Chapel – 'Focus' Vol 8.2

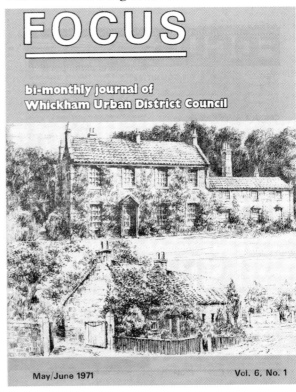

In the July/August 1972 issue we find a 'Get well soon' message to Mr Thomson on his return home from an illness which had occurred whilst he was on holiday in Llandudno. He did return to good health and went on to produce further articles on two subjects, 'Influence of the Church on Medieval Village Life' and 'Friarside Chapel' after this date. Of the 47 issues of the 'Focus' that were published his name appears in some way or other in all but two. On the final occasion he is mentioned in the form of a tribute to him in volume 8, issue number 4, the penultimate edition in November/December 1973. This announced his death on 27th September 1973. Issues of 'Focus' are quite rare these days, fortunately some people collected them and may still have them, but the only copies that I am aware of for use by the public are held in the local studies department at the Gateshead Central Library.

Going to School in the 1930s and early 1940s
by John Mitchell

Whickham Parochial School is the big stone-built building at the top of The Knowles, going up from the Bay Horse pub. It served the village from the 1740s to the early 1970s. The original school founded by Reverend Thomlinson was very small. It was initially a church endowment to educate up to 36 poor village children but later, the building was enlarged during its long lifespan. It was converted after closure in 1972 and became part of the council offices. Thousands of Whickham children have passed through this school during more than two hundred years.

In the 1930s and early '40s, the headmaster was Mr W.W. Rose and he had only two assistant teachers. Miss Best had all of the Infants in one room. Mr Tait had all of the Juniors in another room. The headmaster taught all of the Seniors, full time. There were only three classrooms. They each had very high ceilings and were heated solely by a single open coal fire. There was no school hall. There were no married women teachers in those days. The school leaving age at that time, was 14.

The three teachers had the challenging task of teaching children of different ages, as well as different

The old Parochial School. (Gateshead Libraries)

abilities. Infants were aged 5 to 8; Juniors 9 to 11 and Seniors 12 to 14. Mr Rose and Mr Tait both had a three feet long bamboo cane which they used most days, applied to hands or bottoms, to enforce discipline and to punish misdemeanours. This was common practice in many schools then.

Mr Tait sometimes used to draw a circle on the classroom floor with chalk. If he was in a good mood, it was large – in a bad mood, it was a very small circle. As he taught, he would call out the names of any talkers, or pupils who were not paying attention. If your name was called out, you stood inside the circle. When the circle was so full of 'naughtier,' that their feet protruded over the chalk line of the circle, he walloped all within the circle. When the pupils saw that the circle was almost full, the classroom behaviour and concentration, suddenly improved dramatically.

There were outside toilets. The urinal for the boys was against a tiled wall. On the other side of this wall, were the huge grounds of Colonel Thompson's widow. The boys used to compete with each other to project (pee!) over this wall, into her

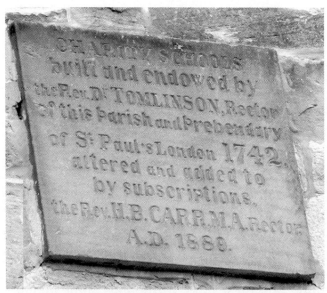

The Plaque showing the date of rebuilding the school. (Richard Pears)

garden. Every summer, on the other side of the urinal wall, in that particularly damp, richly fertilized spot, the lush green weeds grew as high as beanstalks. The toilet seats consisted of three round holes cut into a long, wide, hardwood plank. Impaled on a nail beside each seat was an old hymn book, which served as toilet paper. (It was a Church school!) During most winters, on odd days, the water in the waste trough, which was below the seat holes, was frozen hard. In the bitter winter of 1942, it was a daily problem for long periods. In Winter, when there was snow or slush, and the morning register names were called out, the cry 'no shoes' went up on behalf of quite a few children who were absent because they hadn't adequate footwear. There were some very big families and some very poor families. Some boys had 'basin' haircuts. Unable to afford a barber's costs, their mothers put a basin on their heads and trimmed off any hair which protruded below it. At the other extreme, one boy, an only child, had a father who was a senior Army Officer. The family had a car and a telephone. The boy wore fresh, clean, woollen knee socks, changed every day. At that time, all boys wore short trousers until their teens. The children of these times, passing through the school, had to run the gauntlet through several illnesses that were dangerous then,

before the coming of antibiotics and preventative injections. Scarlet fever, diphtheria, measles, pneumonia, whooping cough, consumption (TB) and even Typhoid, were around then and from time to time, some unfortunate children went down with them.

The penny-stamp playground behind the school was limited in size and far too small for a mix of nearly 150 boisterous children, ranging from tiny five year olds, to big 14s. So the older children had to have the School Lane, The Knowles and the village green as their playground. No supervision. (Imagine that today?) The village green at that time was a mess. It had a scruffy surface

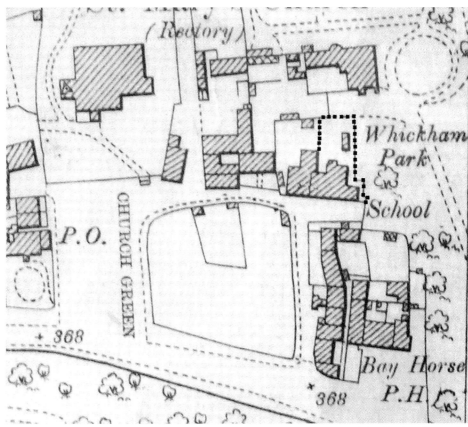

The tiny playground behind the school (outlined in black dots) and the village green can be seen in this 1897 Ordnance Survey map

mix of shale and patchy sparse grass. It was described then by an eminent historian as 'barren'. No lovely flower-beds then – just a rectangular, muddy, mottled space.

The school bell was tolled at the start and end of the playtimes. The old bell remained visible for thirty-odd years after closure but has recently been taken down for some reason. There was a wartime school garden down where the Scouts' Headquarters is now. Mr Rose was a keen gardener and during the war, the boys grew lots of vegetables – 'digging for victory'. In the council office grounds [now the car park] there was an air raid shelter built for the whole school. There were regular air raid practices in it, wearing gas-masks. Wartime rows of Beetroot were grown instead of flowers, in neat, colourful beds, alongside the trimmed Holly and Yew bushes, where the council office car park is today. Potatoes were grown in the Chase Park field.

At the time of Dunkirk, in 1940, on one morning playtime, the children found the village green swarming with weary soldiers, carrying full kit, including their rifles. Apparently the captain of the small ship which rescued them from the beach in France, was told that their regimental barracks was in Wycombe. He had brought them up the Tyne to the only Whickham he knew, by mistake.

19

A wartime jumble sale was once organised and the children were asked to bring items to school. A pair of brothers managed to get a handcart and brought in lots of big loads of really saleable goods and they were praised for this in front of the whole school. That evening, their irate mother dashed down to claim what was left of the large piles of her treasured belongings, which the boys had taken without her permission, whilst she was out at work.

There were no traditional games lessons, because there were no facilities. No hall, no gym, no field. The only Physical Education was 'Drill,' laid down by the 1933 syllabus. In the tiny yard, classes stood in lines and did physical jerks of arms-stretch-knees-bend exercises in unison, on commands of the teacher.

Children attending the school at this time, recognized two important village personalities. Mr Forster was the 'School Board man' and he visited the houses of absentees – always wearing his smart brown military mackintosh. PC Smith was the only village Bobby. Any misbehaviour by village boys, was instantly and permanently cured, by a stern word of warning – accompanied by a clip over the ear, using his gloves.

There were no school meals until the 1944 Act. Most of the village children went home for lunch. During the war, a temporary British Restaurant fed children who lived too far away to go home. It was based in a shop opposite Maughan's Hardware shop (now Newcastle Building Society). Carrot pudding was a regular speciality.

The school 'Library' consisted of a single damp

John Mitchell aged 7

cupboard shelf of about 40 old, stale-smelling books. Every Friday afternoon, the senior children were allowed to choose or change one book and to silently read it for the last hour, while Mr Rose (cane on desk!) completed his weekly returns. They were mostly 'hard' adult-type books with small print and no pictures. No Harry Potter then. Dickens, Kidnapped, Ivanhoe and The Lancers of Lynwood, were well-thumbed favourites of the good readers. Mr Rose was a good teacher. Many things were taught by repetition and 'learning off by heart'. Children chanted Times Tables and were taught traditional poetry and rousing patriotic British songs. Because it was a Church School, learning about Scripture had a disproportionate teaching slot most mornings. Every child who passed through the school, eventually knew that they should never covet their neighbour's ox.

The whole school attended the village church frequently during seasonal festivals and saints' days. The Rector during these years, was the Revd M.H. Huthwaite. Most pupils were scared of him, because he randomly surprised children by asking awkward questions during and after his long, complex sermons. He was old and had a rather forbidding appearance and looked a bit like a white-collared Boris Karloff but he was a nice, kind and generous man. He was an expert Lepidopterist with large, valuable collections of butterflies and moths, all caught and mounted by himself, over his lifetime. In 1972 the old school closed and moved to the new modern building, near The Coachman pub on the Broadway.

The new Parochial School on the Broadway. (Richard Pears)

Beech Grove – An Estate for Professionals
by Jim Ord

At the end of the nineteenth century Whickham was still a rural village, though Swalwell and Dunston had become industrialised. Along the riverside at Dunston were the Atlas rivet works, Dunston Colliery and coal staithes, a saw mill and engine works. Terraced housing was branching out from Ravensworth Road to accommodate the workers for these industries. Swalwell had two collieries, a steelworks, a paper mill on the site of Crowley's eighteenth century mills, a lampblack factory, firebrick works, saw mill and a brewery, and the Delta ironworks at Derwenthaugh. These industries employed many working class people, and a growing number of professionals: managers, engineers, chemists, surveyors, accountants and clerks. Professional families were able to afford better housing and in 1897 seven acres of fields between Whickham and Swalwell at Beech Grove were sold by Sir William Clavering of Axwell to lay out an estate of superior houses.

The 28 houses at Beech Grove were to be on quarter acre plots, the houses to be 'of suitable quality' and costing at least £200 to build with an equivalent sum for gardens, yards, drains and sewers. A few of the houses were built of stone but the majority were of brick construction. A builder Robert Shield of Swalwell provided an estimate in 1897 for a house called Rosecroft. This was for £312, with the actual cost being £317 9s 10d due to some alterations requested by the owner Mr Spencer. The house was lit by gas.

The new streets were named Ashfield Avenue, Beech Avenue, Wallace Avenue and Tyne View Avenue. A new road, Lambton Avenue, was built from Elm Avenue (which connected via Park Drive and Occupation Row with the church green in Whickham village) down to the Beech Grove estate and thence down the hill to connect to Market Lane, the Hexham to Gateshead turnpike road that ran through Swalwell. Elm Avenue and Lambton Avenue were tarmacked but within the Beech Grove estate the roads were surfaced with ash and were not adopted by Whickham Urban District Council. The roads were the responsibility of the house-owners, each being responsible for half of the road along their street frontage.

As expected, the inhabitants of the Beech Grove estate have included business owners, managers, engineers, schoolteachers, doctors, accountants, architects, civil servants and police. There are currently 37 houses on the estate, the additional ones created by building semi-detached rather than detached houses and some infilling on gardens. Although Lambton Avenue has become a busy road, the houses with Beech Grove have managed to retain the semi-rural ambience intended when the estate was laid out.

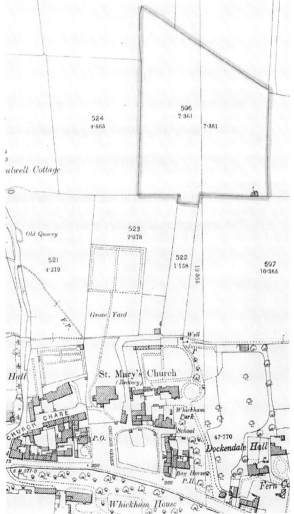

Above: Beech Grove houses. (Richard Pears)

Right: The location of Beech Grove estate, area 596, 1895 Ordnance Survey map.

The Local Co-operative Societies
by Bill Saunders

The idea of working and trading as co-operatives came about in 1760 when many men were unemployed due to the rapid progress of the industrial revolution. Many attempts to form societies in trading, manufacturing and services failed between this date and the 1840s but recent evidence shows that the Fenwick Weavers in Scotland formed a society as early as 1761 and it continued until 1873. It was generally accepted that the Rochdale Society in 1844 was the first successful society but the evidence mentioned above proves otherwise.

Swalwell Co-op Headquarters. (Beamish the Living Museum of the North)

In the north east again there were many attempts at forming societies but it was at Blaydon that the first successful society was formed in 1858, they opened a shop in Cuthbert Street. After this date there was an explosion of successful societies springing up around the area which followed the Rochdale and Blaydon principles which included 'Cash Trading Only' this being the main secret of their success. In Swalwell a society was formed in 1863 and in 1864 shops were opened providing greengroceries, hardware, chilled meats and boot repairing.

The population of Swalwell was about 1,500 at this time. It must be remembered that many of these small societies provided more than goods and foodstuff. They did devote some of their profits

Former Co-operative Societies' Convalescent Home, Gilsland. (Richard Pears)

to benefit the community through providing education for example, the Workers Education Association was founded by the societies collectively in 1903. The Swalwell Society was one of 81 societies to contribute to the building of the Convalescent Home at Gilsland in 1901.

There was no society ever formed in Whickham, however the Swalwell Society in April, 1909 decided to commence the selling of groceries at a branch in Whickham. The shop was opened in May of that year and in April of 1910 an adjacent shop was opened selling draperies and boots. This shop was at the bottom of Fellside Road and may have been site here to serve the mining families of Axwell Park Colliery who lived in the houses of West Street, James Street, George Street, and William Street. It is now a Chinese takeaway and a hairdressers.

When Priestman Collieries opened the new pit at Watergate and built houses for the miners on Broom Lane the Swalwell Industrial Cooperative Society opened a new store including a drapery, grocers and butchers shops.

Economic pressures during the period between the Wars followed by mine closures in the 1960s meant that small societies in mining communities were struggling to survive. The abolition of Retail Price Maintenance in 1964 did not help matters as the independent societies could not compete with the

Whickham Branch of Swalwell Co-op. (Beamish the Living Museum of the North)

high volume 'Stack them High, Sell them Cheap' merchants as they could easily undercut the co-op's prices. Mergers with other small societies was thought to be one solution but it was difficult to convince members to vote for this because they valued the independence of their local societies.

It was inevitable however that change had to happen and in October of 1969 Swalwell (founded 1863), Burnopfield (founded1889), West Stanley (founded1876), Tantobie (founded1861 but had already transfer to West Stanley in 1927) and Craghead & Holmside (founded1883) came together to form the Townley Society. Local readers may remember the Townley Co-op which traded on the Front Street in Whickham but it sadly suffered the same end as many other small shops when the Townley Group was forced with others to transfer their business to the larger North East Co-operative Society in 1982.

Above: The former Swalwell Co-op on Broom Lane. (Bill Saunders)

Right: Townley Co-op branch in Whickham. (Jack Medcalf collection, copyright Whickham LHS)

The Glebe Sports Ground
by Bill Saunders

On 2nd March 1974 saw the opening of the new clubhouse which was a collaboration between the cricket and football clubs and the local council and became a truly dedicated sports facility providing committee room and changing rooms for both the cricket and football teams.

The 1974 clubhouse to the right of the floodlight.

Whickham Cricket Club

Whickham Cricket Club was formed in 1860 and is one of the oldest surviving clubs in the county. Their first recorded fixture was 22nd June 1861 at Winlaton. Whickham scored 33 and 24. In reply Winlaton managed 28 and were 30 for 3.

In 1862 Whickham CC were listed in the famous Lillywhite's Guide. Frederick (Fred) Lillywhite (1829–66) was a sports outfitter and cricketing entrepreneur, who organised the first overseas cricket tour by an English team and published a number of reference works about cricket. In 1848 (still not 20) Fred Lillywhite had produced the first edition of his 'Guide to Cricketers' (known popularly as 'Fred's Guide') which was published until the year of his death in 1866. This was, in many respects, the forerunner of Wisden Cricketers' Almanack

Also in 1862 they spent £5 on equipment and 12 Shillings on ale (nothing new there!). Another match with Winlaton later that year provided the first reference to coloured shirts. 'The gay dresses of the ladies, combined with the white and blue of the cricket, giving the field a picturesque appearance,' was how the scene was described. One early leading bowler was C.R. Carr who had a number of 7 wicket hauls that season.

In 1864 the club was again mentioned in Lillywhite's Guide. The club had 40 members and practised on Mondays, Wednesday, Friday and Saturday. Honorary membership was £1 1 shilling and playing membership was 6 shillings. In 1907 the club became a founder member of the Derwent Valley League becoming champions in 1908.

Whickham Cricket Club in the 1890s.

After the Great War, in 1919, Whickham joined the North Durham Senior League and then in 1920 the Tyne and District league. The following year, 1921 they returned to the North Durham Senior league and remained there until the league was suspended due to the Second World War. In the final season of 1939 Whickham were crowned champions.

After the Second World War the club were admitted to the Northern Combination in 1947 and were champions in their first season. In 1950 the club was admitted to the

North West Durham League when the league was extended to 12 clubs and remained there for the next 35 years.

In 1974 Whickham won their first North West Durham Championship. The following year, Whickham retained the championship, Kelvin Ashley scoring 106 against Craghead and Jackie King scoring 101 not out against Clara Vale.

The new millennium saw the merger of the TSL with the Northumberland league to form the Northumberland and Tyneside Senior league (NTSL). Season 2000 saw 20 teams compete.

The top 10 would make up division 1 and the bottom 10 division 2 with a system of promotion and relegation. Whickham had an excellent season finishing in 4th thus ensuring top flite status.

The old pavilion

The year 2010 – the club's 150th year – was an excellent one. The First XI were in contention for promotion till the last few weeks finishing in third place. The under 15s

remained unbeaten throughout the league season finishing runners up to Greenside and were also winners in the Willis Elliot Cup. As part of the celebrations during their 150th year, a match was organised at Beamish Museum against Percy Main Cricket Club who were also in their 150th year. The game was played to 1860 rules which were rather complicated and totally different to those played today. Both players and spectators were dressed in typical Victorian costume for the occasion which created a wonderful atmosphere and a spectacular scene. Also in August of that year the club hosted a team from the MCC, which included former Whickham player James Pearce in their side. Whickham Cricket Club have played their all their 150 plus years of cricket at the Glebe ground which has seen some great days and provided cricketing and social opportunities for generations.

Left: The 150th anniversary match.

Whickham Football Club

Research has revealed that organised football was played in and around Whickham from about 1901. Below is an extract from 1901-02 (possibly 1902-03) with a Whickham team shown in 5th position in the Northern Combination League, which consisted of 12 other clubs.

Pos		Pl	W	D	L	GF	GA	Pts
5	WHICKHAM	23	10	5	8	60	52	25

The Club has photographs of a team named Whickham AFC during the early twentieth century with one precisely dated 1905-06. Again photographic evidence shows that a club named Axwell Park Rovers were also active between 1904 and 1924 but they were based in Swalwell, this can cause some confusion between the two as one reads on.

No evidence has emerged to show that a football club under the name of Whickham FC played in organised leagues between the two wars. It would appear that the Whickham Club

Whickham Football Club 1905-06.

was in effect reformed in 1944, the nickname allegedly appended to it of the 'Home Guard Club' is now thought to be a myth. In 1950-51 the club moved to their current Glebe Ground home to share with Whickham Cricket Club. At this point in time the name was changed Axwell Park Colliery Welfare. The NCB, owners of the land, expressed concerns that operating as Whickham FC gave the club no recognisable links with local pits or coalmining so the name of Axwell Park CW was used to appease the NCB and to allow the club to play on the Glebe Ground. In 1968 the ground was bought from the National Coal Board by the Local Council.

League History

In 1944 they played in the Derwent Valley League, before moving to the Northern Combination in the early 1970s, then to the Wearside League in 1974. Whickham enjoyed quite a degree of success at this level before joining the Northern League Second Division in 1988. After just one season in the Second Division under the management of Billy Hodgson the club gained promotion for the first time into the First Division in 1988-89 and spent three seasons there before being relegated in 1991-92. Another promotion came in 1994-95 and a further two seasons were spent in the 1st Division before another relegation in 1996-97 back into the Second Division where they have since remained.

Cup Success

The Football Association Challenge Vase, commonly referred to as the FA Vase, is a nationwide knockout cup competition. It was staged for the first time 1974-75, effectively replacing the FA Amateur Cup which was discontinued after the abolition of official amateur status by the FA.

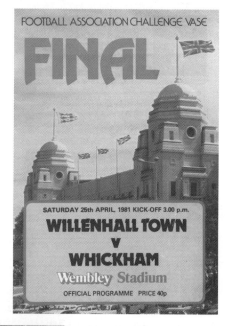

Whickham reached the semi-final of the FA Vase in 1978-79 losing to Almondsbury Greenway but it was in 1981 that Whickham had their finest hour. After a titanic struggle to overcome Windsor & Eton in the semi-final, they faced Willenhall, a midlands club, under the Twin Towers of Wembley in the final.

An estimated 5,000 fans followed Whickham to Wembley and in a gripping match they saw Whickham come back from 2-0 down to level at 2-2 at full time with goals from Alan Scott and Ronnie Williamson. The game went into extra-time during which Billy Cawthra broke away to score the winner making it 3-2 and the Vase was on its way to Tyneside. The success in 1981 has left Whickham FC with a unique place in history as being the last north east based club to win in a national final at the old Wembley Stadium which is of course now re-built. Whickham again nearly reached Wembley in 1983-84 before losing in their semi-final against Stansted.

Above: The programme for the FA Vase final in 1981.

Left: The Whickham team celebrate winning the FA Vase at Wembley.

The team returning to Whickham with the FA Vase. (Jack Medcalf collection, copyright Whickham LHS)

The Durham Challenge Cup was first contested in 1884 and is Durham County's most prestigious trophy. In 2006 after an impressive run, including wins over four First Division teams, Whickham found themselves in the final against Billingham Synthonia at Ferens Park, Durham. Whickham were second best for long periods against a very good Billingham side but against all the odds, two late goals from Kenny Boyle and Ian Robson snatched victory for Whickham.

The following season, 2007, Whickham continued their cup success by winning the newly named Ernest Armstrong Memorial Cup (Second Division Cup) by defeating Penrith in an exciting penalty shoot-out.

The Football Club Badge.

Until the appearance of Whickham FC in the FA Vase Final of 1981, the club did not have a club badge. It was at the request of the FA that the Vase finalists should have a club badge on their shirts. This request prompted the then club secretary Jackie Gilbert to quickly create a design and as Lang Jack was part of Whickham Folklore his image was chosen to feature on the badge along with the date of foundation in 1944. As mentioned earlier this date has now been proved to be when the club was reformed.

Above all else Whickham Football Club to this day has a reputation throughout the north east as being a friendly club run by a group of honest and hardworking people. With young players in the team who play for the enjoyment of the game and are not driven by the prospect of financial gain as is the case with football generally today.

Information and pictures with the kind permission of Whickham Cricket Club and Football Club. Transcribed and edited by Bill Saunders.

Henzell's Tea Shop and Grocers
by Helen Page

Until the late 1970s the northern side of Whickham Front Street was lined with houses and shops. In the nineteenth century one of those shops was Henzell's. William Milburn Henzell (1825-1891) was descended from the Huguenot families who fled religious persecution in France in the 1600s. The Henzell, Tysack and Tittery families were glassmakers who settled in Newcastle, where they set up business in the Ouseburn area.

William opened a grocers shop in 1849 on Front Street, Whickham, which in the nineteenth century was a thriving agricultural and mining community. He lived in Elswick, Newcastle, with his wife Jane (née Stephenson) and their five children and two servants. He was described as 'tea maker and grocer' in the 1861, 1871 and 1881 censuses. In 1881 he employed six men and four boys. His eldest son John was

'Henzell's First Class Teas'. (Helen Page)

described as a 'grocer and tea dealer manager'. Another son, Charles, aged fifteen, was a 'grocer's apprentice'. His two other sons, William and Robert, were a 'merchant's clerk' and an 'oil merchant' respectively, and thus not employed in the family business.

William carried on the business until his death in 1891. The shop was situated on the Front Street, almost opposite the present telephone exchange. When the shop under the name Henzell's was closed is unknown, though in 1911 William's son John lived in Dunston with his wife and four daughters and his occupation was still 'grocer', but he was described as a 'commercial traveller'. His wife was Principal of a private girls' school and his daughters were teachers.

William Milburn Henzell was a very influential man; he founded the Newcastle Hospital for Incurables and was Chairman of the Hospital for Diseases of the Chest. He was a member of Newcastle Town Council and the Board of Governors, a member of the Free Library Committee and Governor of the Grammar School. He also founded Liddle, Henzell & Co. glass and flint bottle works near Ouseburn Bridge, Byker. They manufactured glass until 1934. Some of the furnace arches can still be seen along the footpath by the side of the Ouseburn, with fused flint and other materials embedded in the brickwork. His address was given as 42 Clayton Street, Newcastle, in the 'London Gazette' of 5th October 1886.

The Whickham shop changed hands several times until it eventually became Lily Butler's dress shop, adjacent to the post office. These shops and the surrounding houses were demolished to make way for the St Mary's Green shopping centre in the 1970s.

Henzell's shop prior to demolition. (Jack Medcalf collection, copyright Whickham LHS)

Diary of a Sun Vitesse Bicycle
by Ethel Armstrong

The bicycle was first bought in the early part of 1939 and was supplied by Robertsons of Peterborough. It has been in the owner's possession since she was 11 years old. At the time it was a bit unusual as bikes were mostly black in those days and it has handlebars which can be turned over to give a shallow drop and the front forks are of solid stainless steel. It also has a two speed gear. Most ordinary bikes then were of the 'sit up and beg' type. It has always been treasured and valued because the money to buy such things took a lot of raising and not easily come by at the time.

It was used daily to go to school etc as buses were few and far between. At around April 1940 my parents moved to Gateshead, leaving me and my brother at Peterborough with friends to complete the school term. The war was going badly and in June 1940, after the capitulation of France, invasion was imminent and without warning my Mother arrived and we were whisked north to Gateshead, travelling in the cab of an open truck with furniture and bikes on the back. Covered by a tarpaulin and tied down with ropes which unfortunately chaffed the bike causing a black mark on the frame.

The bike resumed school duty but within three weeks a bomb was dropped near the Tyne Bridge and for the second time the school was evacuated to Wensleydale in Yorkshire and later the bike was sent by train. It was in daily use again and stored in a stone barn. After a change of billet its home was a wooden barn. At no time was it ever stored in the open. It did have a slight accident when in Yorkshire, when it scraped against the stone parapet of a bridge. It was checked for a possible buckled front wheel but found to have no damage.

Ethel on her new bike, 1939.

After a year, in June 1941, it came back to Gateshead on the train with the owner and was used once more for school, general purposes and leisure with a few longer journeys. It was twice pedalled to Yorkshire and back, County Durham and Northumberland.

In the 1960s as the owner became older and busier and the traffic heaver as new faster motorways appeared, it was used less often. This stopped altogether when a car was bought in the late 1960s. It came to Whickham in 1971, after the owner's marriage and has been subjected to changes in climate and temperature. It has been brought out occasionally for attention to tyres, oil and cleaning. It was professionally serviced in the 1980s when new tyres, brake blocks and mudguards were fitted.

During the war the bike had to be used with a fixed gear as the two speed gear failed and could not be replaced until these items became available again. The four speed gear was fitted about 1948. The saddlebag was of an earlier date, having been on the owner's mother's bike in the early 1930s. The dynamo was from father's bike bought in the 1950s.

On the frame, below the saddle, there was a security locking system device which prevents the back wheel being removed, when the bike is left parked in public. It was activated by clicking the arms of the device together and removing the key. The bike is now in need of 'TLC' but useable and is still very dear to the owner, who would like it to go to a good home where it would be loved and looked after. It is now 73 years old and it would be sad if it ended up on the scrap heap.

Written by Ethel Armstrong just prior to the bike and story were donated to Beamish Museum.

Ethel and her bike in the 1970s.

Whickham Orchard
by John Mitchell

As late as the 1930s and '40s, 'the orchard' was still a thriving, viable business. Orchards were ten-a-penny and to be expected in places like Kent, Worcester and Hereford, but a large orchard in the cold north east, a few hundred feet above sea level, was a most unlikely setting and was unusual.

An important necessity for successful fruit-growing, is a frost-free mild Spring, when the vulnerable fruit blossom is blooming. The better the Spring weather, the better the insect pollination and the better the eventual fruit crop. Whickham gets more than its fair share of frosts and cold east winds and Sea Fret every spring. There is evidence to show that the orchard was there in the 1600s and in spite of these negative conditions, our village orchard has churned out quality fruits for hundreds of years.

Only a token legacy of the whole original large orchard remains as a frontage now.

The original land occupied nearly three acres and stretched well down Duckpool Lane and is now covered by a good number of houses, which make up the eponymous Orchard Estate. The owners were the Turnbulls, an affluent family who have lived in Whickham for generations and owned land and several properties. The site of the current council offices was originally land owned by the Turnbulls. Grandad Turnbull, in the 1890s, used to go down to Swalwell Railway station by Tom Easy's horse and carriage and then on to Scotland for his annual Grouse shooting.

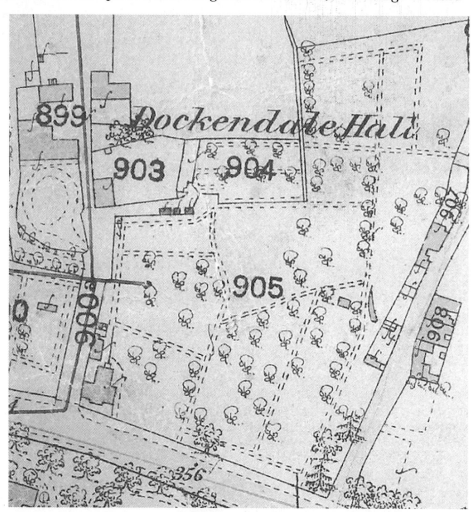

Map of the Orchard, area 905, in 1856. (Ordnance Survey)

The orchard had stone-built fruit storage sheds from which they sold their tree crops of plums, damsons, apples and pears. The plums and damsons were sold as soon as they were ripe. The pears, and the cooking and eating apples were skillfully packed and stored in trays in the stone sheds. There were many different old English varieties, with varied names, colours and flavours. You could opt for fruit for immediate use or 'good keepers'. They were then sold steadily, way beyond Christmas and, in a good year, sometimes up to Easter. They sold very small tasty pears, locally called 'Green Jacks' – four for a halfpenny! In early spring, they sold large quantities of rhubarb and mint. They provided rhubarb for most of the Tyneside Co-op shops.

In early summer, they sold lots and lots of Gooseberries, which grew under the trees. During the two World Wars, when food was short and imported fruits were virtually non-existent, the village orchard was still able to supply local people with tasty treats.

Staff outside the Whickham branch of Swalwell Co-op, Fellside Road. (Beamish the Living Museum of the North)

The Turnbulls' house was originally a toll-house and it was very small. The two new buildings (Vets and bungalow) were added after the Second World War. From the gateway of the original stone toll-house, old Mr Turnbull, who was confined to a wheelchair in his later years, served his customers. In winter, he was swathed in warm clothing and wore woolen mitts on his old hands. In his front window, he had a large glass-topped case, displaying his considerable collection of wild birds' eggs, which he had acquired in his youth.

His son Bill returned from the war as an RAF officer, along with his attractive wife-to-be, who was a WREN. They made a handsome, striking pair, both in their smart uniforms, regularly walking arm in arm through the then traffic-free village. Later, they opened a popular general dealer's shop (now Vets) on the site, which was greatly appreciated for a few years but sadly missed when it closed.

Modern supermarkets sell shiny symmetrical fruits without any visible imperfections. Whickham Orchard fruits sometimes had the odd skin blemish and some were slightly misshapen. However, one thing you could be sure of, Whickham Orchard fruits were very tasty and always completely free of any modern residual pesticides or herbicides.

The Turnbulls' house. (Richard Pears)

The Parish Church of St Mary the Virgin
by Wendy Oloman

The church is set in a prominent position looking north over the Tyne valley and south over the older part of the village. On the north the valley sides drop steeply away down the Banky Fields where the early drift mines produced the coal which brought wealth to our area. In ancient times it is likely that there were few if any trees on these slopes and the church would stand out to any passing along the valley and also a landmark easily seen from Newcastle. It has Norman origins but

View of the Church c. 1900. (Gateshead Libraries)

there may have been an earlier structure, although no trace remains. The first rector recorded was Alan in 1200 but the earliest record of a church was c. 1220.

From the outside St Mary's is an attractive but simple sandstone building with a square tower at the west end and a deep porch on the south. However what we see now is the result of a long life of changes and alterations with a disastrous fire in 1841 which nearly destroyed the church. The 'Newcastle Chronicle' reported:

On Sunday afternoon last (14th November) the ancient and beautiful church of Whickham was nearly destroyed by fire. It appears that the flues from the stoves had become overheated and had set fire to the fittings up of one of the pews, and the conflagration so far gained a head that the flames burnt from the roof. The Revd Robert Chatto, the clergyman of the parish endeavoured to gain an entrance to the door but without effect. The parish engine was procured but on its arrival it appeared it had been so long out of use, it would not act. A second engine was obtained but similar success. The inhabitants at length effected an entrance by breaking the north windows, and by dint of perseverance and the most laudable exertions the fire was subdued. We understand about eighty pews were destroyed.

Following this there was a major renovation by the architect Anthony Salvin. The nave is the oldest part of the church with the chancel arch dating to the mid-twelfth century. The arch is semicircular and rests on scalloped cushion capitals. Towards the end of that century the south four bay aisle was added in the Transitional style. The similar north aisle was rebuilt after the fire with another aisle added in 1861-2. By the nineteenth century there were box pews in the nave and also galleries with access stairs at the west end but those that were not damaged by the fire were removed in the 1861-2 renovation.

The chancel also appears to date from the twelfth century with a priest's door on the

Revd Robert Thomlinson.

south side. The reredos behind the altar was added in the nineteenth century. The twelfth century font situated at the west end under the tower is made of Frosterley marble. The tower was probably built in the fourteenth century. Like many towers in the northern counties it may have been partly defensive as the only original access into the ringing chamber and belfry was by ladder from the inside of the church and the door can still be seen above the baptistry. In the nineteenth century an exterior staircase was built on the north side of the tower.

All the stained glass in the church dates from the nineteenth and twentieth centuries and includes one designed by William Morris and one by William Wailes. There are several striking modern windows. Among the monuments inside is one in the chancel to the Reverend Robert Thomlinson (1668-1747), who came to Whickham in 1712.

He disliked the old rectory next to the church so in 1713 he built a new rectory (now the health centre) on the glebe lands at the corner of the Front Street and Rectory Lane. The former rectory became a private house, but returned to use as the Rectory in 1922. Thomlinson founded the parochial school next to the church in 1742. He was a great bibliophile and his collection was so valuable that Sir Walter Blackett of Wallington built a new library to house Thomlinson's books on the side of St Nicholas's Cathedral in Newcastle. The books were transferred there on Thomlinson's death and are now in Newcastle City Library.

Left: Thomlinson's new Rectory of 1713, now the Health Centre. (Richard Pears)

Below: The arms of Lord Crewe, Prince Bishop of Durham, with Thomlinson's arms below.

The graveyard is all round the church with the southern part being the oldest part. There are grave stones dating back to 1626 and show victims of the plague, evidence of skirmishes with the Scots, a soldier of Cromwell (both soldiers and horses were billeted in the church), mining deaths and many interesting villagers. The Carr-Ellison family of Dunston Hill have a vault and George Bowes of Gibside (1701-1760) was buried at Whickham until the building of his Chapel and mausoleum at Gibside was completed. There is a memorial to the composer William Shield (1752-1829) born in Swalwell and buried in Westminster Abbey.

The most spectacular monument is to Harry Clasper (1812-1870) a world champion rower and boat builder. He improved racing boat design with outriggers, shell hulls and sliding seats. Several thousand people took part in his funeral procession from Newcastle to Whickham where his statue now looks down to the river Tyne. Local legend says that if you walk round it three times he will come down and chase you. His mother's memorial stone nearby is shaped as half a racing scull.

Apart from the man-made features one of the most wonderful is the mass of snowdrops that grow under the trees on the north side of the church which is rarely seen by the casual passer-by.

St Mary the Virgin was the only Anglican church in Whickham parish until the 1870s when new churches were built in other villages. Christ Church in Dunston opened in 1873 (demolished 1976), St Cuthbert's Church in Marley Hill opened in 1877 and Holy Trinity Church in Swalwell in 1905.

William Shield.

Harry Clasper monument.

Methodism in Whickham and District
by Richard Pears

John Wesley introduced Methodism to Whickham parish. The first visit in November 1742 was inauspicious (John Welsey in his diary noted that those who heard him at Whickham were 'dead, senseless and unaffected'), but in April 1747 he had a favourable reception at Swalwell, preaching there again in 1757 and in 1759. Those wishing to hear him in 1759 were so great that barely a third could fit into the room, so the Presbyterian minister Revd E. Arthur offered Wesley the use of the Ebenezer Presbyterian Chapel (opened in 1750, demolished in 1976). Wesley had returned to Whickham in 1752, preaching 'at Mrs Armstrong's door' (at the bottom of Broom Lane).

The audience were more favourable and the Anglican rector, Revd Williamson, was a friend of the Wesleys. There was a Methodist preaching-house in Whickham in 1790 and another in Swalwell in 1799. Methodism divided after the Wesleys' deaths into Wesleyan and Primitive Methodists (they reunited in 1932), and in Whickham and neighbouring villages there were often chapels built for both congregations. A Welseyan Methodist Chapel opened on Market Lane, Swalwell, in 1817 and a Primitive Methodist community was there in 1824.

Above: Cottages at junction of Broom Lane and Front Street where Wesley preached. (Richard Pears)

Right: Fellside Road Wesleyan Methodist Chapel. (Bill Saunders)

The Wesleyan Methodists built a new chapel at the foot of Fellside Road in 1869. They moved to a new Chapel on Ancaster Road in 1980. The new Primitive Methodist Church that opened on Whickham Front Street in 1871 was named the Spoor Memorial Chapel after Joseph Spoor (1813-69) a preacher who was born in Whickham.

In Swalwell the Wesleyan Methodists moved to a new Chapel on Market Lane in 1930. This is now a nursery.

Above: Reverend Joseph Spoor.

Right: Swalwell Methodist Chapel. (Richard Pears)

In Dunston the first Methodist meetings were held in Bute Hall, a farmhouse near the coal staithes. A Wesleyan Methodist Chapel was built in Stokoe Square in 1877, replaced by a new building on Hexham Road in 1903. The Primitive Methodists opened a chapel in the Great Square and moved to premises in Ravensworth Road in the later nineteenth century. When these became too small they sold their chapel the Salvation Army in 1906 and bought a chapel from the Independent Methodists in Wood Street. They moved again to Dunston Hill Methodist Church in 1963. A Methodist New Connexion Chapel opened in Ravensworth Road, Dunston. This became Ravensworth Road Chapel, but was demolished in 2001. Today another small Methodist community meets in Ravensworth Road, close to first meeting place in Dunston.

Sunniside Chapel. (Beamish the Living Museum of the North)

In 1837 a Primitive Methodist Chapel opened in Sunniside. This was replaced by a new building in 1910, which is still in use. A Primitive Methodist Chapel opened in 1853 to serve the mining families of Marley Hill, but it was demolished along with the houses of Chapel Row in 1936. There was also a Wesleyan Chapel. The photograph left and the map below show how the chapels and houses were located right next to the colliery.

Above: Chapel Row and houses in Marley Hill. (Beamish the Living Museum of the North)

Right: 1897 map showing Primitive and Wesleyan Methodist Chapels at Marley Hill Colliery. (Ordnance Survey)

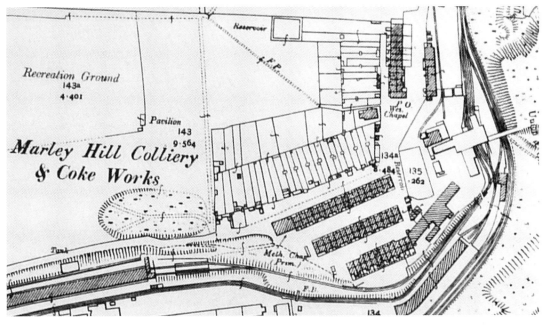

St Mary's RC Church and School, Dockendale
by Thelma Rix

After the Reformation there was little evidence of Catholicism in Whickham, although there were isolated references. In 1569, after the unsuccessful rebellion of the Earls of Westmorland and Northumberland, two Catholic men were hanged on Church Green. On 13th June 1584 Nicholas Barrass, son of Anthony Barrass of Whickham was ordained priest at Soissons, in France after studying at Reims and Douai, so the faith had managed to survive. Sacred Heart Roman Catholic Church opened in Byermoor in 1876 and St Philip Neri Church, Dunston, opened in 1882 (rebuilt 1905). The first Mass in Whickham since the Reformation was said sometime between June and October 1944, when priests from Dunston said Sunday Mass in the County School (now known as Whickham Front Street School). An altar and the vestments were kept in a large locked cupboard in the hall, for a fee of £1 per week paid to Durham Education Authority.

On 3rd June 1947 the Catholic Church authorities bought Dockendale Hall to be a presbytery. The old stables were converted into the new church of St Mary's. On 24th August 1948 the parish was established by Bishop McCormack, Bishop of Hexham and Newcastle, with Fr Leo Pickering as the first Priest. The church was officially blessed on 3rd May 1949.

Whickham remained a small village (there were 250 in the original parish) until 1958 when there was a big increase in the house building programme. In 1961 Bishop Cunningham insisted, 'Something must be done immediately to make more provision for the parishioners.' The result was an extension to the church known as St Joseph's Chapel. It was officially opened and blessed by the Bishop on 16th July 1962.

As the population grew a new church was needed and Dockendale Hall to be sold to raise money. On 13th November 1972, W.A. & R. Johnson of Willington, Crook, started building the new church and presbytery. The presbytery was ready on Wednesday, 29th August 1973 and the official opening and blessing of the church was carried out by Bishop Hugh Lindsay on 8th September 1973 at a Concelebrated Mass with Fathers Clark, O'Neill, Timney, Walsh, Gerard McClean and Vincent McClean.

Old RC Church. (Richard Pears)

Parish Priests

Father Leo Pickering: 24th August 1948 – 23rd March 1953.

Father J. McKeown: managed the parish from 26th March 1953 – 12th August 1953.

Father James Farrow: August 1953 – 15th August 1957.

Father Vincent McClean: August 1957 – November 1980.

Father John Taggart: November 1980 – September 1995.

Father Michael Hickey: September 1995 – 2003.

Served from Lobley Hill

Father Michael Humble Humble: 2003 – 2011

Father Jeffrey Dodds: 2011.

(Retired priests in residence: Father Joseph Travers and Father Michael McKenna.)

New RC Church. (Richard Pears)

Right: Father Pickering and Father McKeown graves. (Richard Pears)

The School

Catholic Education began in Whickham in the house of Mr and Mrs McWilliams of Eleanor Terrace. Father Walsh came up from Dunston and gave instructions to the children who attended the County School. Anyone who wanted their children to go to a Catholic School had to send them to the Sacred Heart, Byermoor, St Philip Neri's, Dunston or St Joseph's, Blaydon.

When Father Pickering founded the parish it was with the intention of founding a school also, but it was not until 1970 that Mr Edward Short, the Minister for Education, instructed Miss Alice Bacon (Parliamentary Secretary to the DES – Department of Education and Science) to inform the Bishop that the new school had been put on the Design List.

On 31st March 1971 Minto Construction Company started to build. Not long after the commencement, Mr Matlock, the quantity Surveyor, died, then Minto Construction went bankrupt. New plans had to be drawn up and it looked as if the school would be delayed indefinitely. However, Mr Rossi, the architect, was a college friend of the chief architect at the DES, whose mother lived in Whickham. An excited Mr Rossi rang up and said, 'The DES Architect has come to Whickham today and is coming to the presbytery tonight.' All correspondence was duly signed that night, saving months of delay.

St Mary's RC School. (Richard Pears)

After a long illness, Mr Rossi, the architect, died and Mr J. Temple, who was a fellow architect with Mr Rossi, left the firm, but with a new architect, Mr Wilf McCann, and the building firm of Mr Reg Hattam of Birtley, the school opened on 10th April 1972.

Head Teachers

Mr Leo Mason: 1972 – 1985

Mr Arthur Burke: 1985 – 1998

Mrs Mary McMillan: 1998 – 2015

Mr Joe Wheatley: 2015 –

Dockendale Hall
by Thelma Rix

Dockendale Hall. (Bill Saunders)

Dockendale Hall was built during the late sixteenth century and is one of the oldest buildings in Whickham Village. Dockendale originally belonged to the Earl of Darlington. There is a record in the Ryton Register of a Silvertop of Dockendale Hall who died in a ferry accident on the River Tyne. The ferry could have been one which belonged to an Arthur Swinburn of Blaydon who in 1593 paid to the Rector of Ryton, 2d in tithes, for a boat, which was possibly a ferry boat. In the accident 18 people were drowned. The Ryton Register states the names of the people and where they lived. The Silvertops were an important Catholic family at the time. It is reputed that Oliver Cromwell stayed at Dockendale Hall when his army camped in Whickham for two days on their march to Edinburgh in 1648. Cromwell was known to humiliate his enemies by taking over their homes. The owner of the Hall at the time was Sir Thomas Liddell of Ravensworth. He was a Royalist who had supported King Charles I by keeping Newcastle a Royalist stronghold during the occupation by the Scots in 1640. He also defended Newcastle during the siege in 1644.

Statue of Oliver Cromwell at Houses of Parliament, London. (Richard Pears)

A woman who lived in Dockendale Hall in 1760 bought a bureau at a sale at the Blacksmith's Arms, in Blaydon. She paid 4s 6d for it as it was not in very good condition. One of her neighbours helped her to take it to Whickham. As they were doing so, some gold fell out, which they quickly hid. They got some more people to help them, who reported hearing a rattle inside the bureau. The neighbour, who was a nailer, said it was just loose nails. Back at Whickham the lady and the nailer dismantled the bureau and found a large quantity of gold. The woman gave the nailer £200, which was enough to buy a house and a shop. No one knew where the gold had come from, but the bureau had belonged to a wealthy Newcastle family in 1715 and none of the gold was later than the reign of James II (1685-88).

Very little is known of the Hall until the nineteenth century when there is a record of a John Meek, a local farmer, who lived in Dockendale Hall. Not much is known about him but he lived there until his death in 1840. In 1841 Thomas Taylor took over the holding on the Hall. He made several alterations and after his death the Misses Taylors continued to live there until the beginning of the century.

Mr Campbell was the next owner, whose son unsuccessfully tried to raise pedigree cattle. The bank took over the estate dond sold it to a Canon Phelps. After the death of Canon Phelps and his widow, the estate was purchased by the Catholic Church Authority in 1947. Extensive rebuilding made the stables into the Catholic Church and Dockendale Hall into the presbytery. The tithes on Dockendale Hall Estate were extinguished by the Tithes Redemption Commission as from 2nd October 1949.

Ralph Carr of Dunston Hill House
by Bill Saunders

Those readers who have at some time passed along the Whickham Highway between Whickham and Gateshead may have noticed the vast change which has taken place by the building of new homes on the site of the old Dunston Hill Hospital The hospital stood within the grounds of what once was a magnificent private estate dominated by the country house. The house was once used as the administration block of the hospital but now been renovated and converted into styish apartment dwellings.

It is the country house and the people who first lived there that my story revolves. The building which stands today can be safely dated about 1740, however it is

Dunston Hill House. (Richard Pears)

thought that the rear section of the building may have been built between 1667 and 1739. The Dunston Hill Estate, formerly owned by the Shafto family was purchased by John Carr in 1704. John Carr, was a mining engineer in Cumberland and Westmoreland and was also an agent to Lord Thanet and the Claverings of Axwell among others. He was married to Sarah, daughter of William Wynne of Gateshead, John Carr died in 1739 and is buried in Whickham Churchyard. The house was inherited by his son Ralph and it is Ralph who is the main character in my story. The historian, Richard Welford (late nineteenth century) in his chapter about Ralph Carr in 'Men of Mark Twixt Tyne and Tweed', tells us *'Of some good men's lives ample details are forthcoming; of others only meagre details are obtainable; of many there is no record at all. In this last-named category comes a remarkable man, who occupied a leading position in Newcastle during the greater part of the last century.'*

Ralph Carr was born 22nd September 1711, and was the ninth of twelve children, six of his brothers and sisters died between the ages of 22 and 42. On the 17th October 1729 he was apprenticed to Matthew Bowes, merchant adventurer and boothman or corn merchant. On completion of his apprenticeship he travelled through Holland, Germany and on to the Baltic, he spent some time in the newly founded city of St Petersburg. His travels done, young Ralph started his business career in 1737 as a general merchant in Newcastle. Trading in coal, iron, timber, corn, glass, alum, wines and spirits as well as tea, butter, tobacco and snuff, no area of business held any fears for him. He also had interests overseas in plantations in America and the Far East and also acted as an insurance broker for shipping. A man of considerable business acumen.

Ralph Carr.

Map of Dunston Hill estate in the 1890s. (Ordnance Survey)

On inheriting the family home at Dunston Hill, in 1739 Ralph enlarged the house and extended the boundaries of the estate where he lived for many years while still a bachelor. By 1745 Ralph Carr had become such a wealthy man that he was called upon by the government of the day to help out in a crisis. The crisis in question was the Young Pretender, Charles Edward Stuart, he had landed in Scotland and proceeded to gather support. He gained control of Edinburgh and soon after on 21st September 1745 defeated the army of General Cope, Commander in Chief in Scotland, at Preston Pans. This caused great consternation throughout England and at Newcastle in particular. By October 29th, General Wade had arrived in Newcastle with an army of about 12 to 13,000 men en route to Scotland. An embarrassing situation now arose, because of the shortage of coin there was not enough money to pay the troops stationed at Newcastle. This was when the assistance of Ralph Carr was sought. As he was probably one of the few men in the north east to have the ready cash available and he was requested to act as government banker of troop payments. No doubt Ralph Carr charged interest on the money he advanced and made a tidy profit. Some years later it was suggested to him by Mr John Campbell, his London agent that he open a bank in Newcastle. His experience of 1745 may have helped encourage him in this direction and in 1755 he and three partners opened the first bank in Newcastle. The four gentlemen, the others being Joseph Airey, Matthew Bell and John Cookson each invested £500 in the venture and opened premises at the residence of Joseph Airey in Pilgrim Street, Newcastle. This it would appear was a temporary address for the bank as the public were informed by both the 'Newcastle Courant' and the 'Newcastle Journal' on 22nd November 1755 that *'Notice is hereby given that the Newcastle Bank will be opened on Monday next, at the house late Mr Robinson's, in Pilgrim Street, where all Business in the Banking and Exchange Way will be transacted as in London.'*

While there were provincial banks in other parts of the country, notably Woods at Gloucester and Samuel Smith at Nottingham it is thought that the premises in Pilgrim Street was the first in England solely dedicated to the business of banking, it became known locally as the 'Old Bank'. It seems that the services of the bank were quite varied, the next item may surprise a few readers, the 'Newcastle Journal' of 8th September 1759 carried the news that *'Any person wanting tickets in the present State Lottery may be supplied at the Newcastle Bank on the same terms as at London.'* There really is nothing new, is there?

challenging time. Our extended Company were working together, on-stage, back-stage, front-of-house, and the people of Whickham and surrounding areas supporting us. Settled in our permanent home in the heart of Whickham, we became more ambitious, presenting plays, musicals ('Salad Days', 'Good Companions', 'Anything Goes', 'Stepping Out', etc) revues. Then a pantomime each Christmas, which became a village tradition, attracting families from a much wider area.

Panto involved all members of the Theatre Club in all aspects of 'putting on a show':

1. Set designers, scenery painters and builders.
2. Costume designers and makers.
3. Props designers and craftsmen.
4. Local musicians.
5. Local dance schools.
6. Student groups.
7. Permanent professional lighting expert.
8. Front-of-house Manager and helpers.
9. Refreshment volunteers, always ready with the welcome 'cuppa' during rehearsals and shows.

'Humpty Dumpty' Christmas pantomime, 1991. (Pam Neville)

The club's main objectives were always to produce shows of a high standard, and to entertain our audiences. That took a lot of hard work, time, commitment, some tears, but a lot of fun and laughter and camaraderie. We wanted to be an integral part of our community, which we did by working with our local churches to produce plays at Eastertime and perform them in St Mary's Church, with great support from the clergy and parishioners. A few examples: T.S. Elliot's 'Murder in the Cathedral', 'Joseph and his Technicolor Dreamcoat', 'Godspell', culminating in our Millennium production, the Passion Play 'Time Lord 2000' staged in Chase Park on a lovely evening on 15th April, bringing together all the churches of Whickham. A large cast, musicians, sound engineers, lighting team, wardrobe team, stewards – and, oh, yes, horses and a huge audience. Fortunately a dry evening, and a magnificent sunset over Whickham for our final scene 'The Resurrection.' A uniting, emotional, thrilling and rewarding time for all.

'Timelord 2000' in Whickham Chase Park. (David Rix)

Whickham Theatre Club continued performing until 2015, with an annual programme of plays, revues, musicals, pantomimes. We said our goodbyes to members and welcomed new ones. There has always remained a nucleus of those people who gathered in that house in 1976. Lifetime friendships had been forged, and a lifetime of bringing entertainment to Whickham. And so … **The Curtain Falls.**

The Dunston Rocket
by Richard Pears

During the 1960s Whickham Urban District Council sought to increase the number of dwellings in Dunston, the most populous area of the District. The area had many Victorian terraces of houses, flats and shops. The plan called for 400 housing units, varying in size from single person ownership to family accommodation. The area earmarked for development, some 14 acres, was restricted by a railway embankment on one side, a gas works on the other and existing streets including Ravensworth Road and Ellison Road. The ground was poor and the water table was close to ground level. The Council tried to avoid the common solution of the 1960s to build slabs of high rise flats, recognising

Council model (from Whickham 'Focus' magazine March/April 1967).

even then the social problems that could develop in these buildings. The necessity of incorporating precious green space, preventing car parks dominating open areas and the number of homes required obliged the Council to include one major tower block in the scheme, with other accommodation in blocks of 4 or 5 stories. This would be Derwent Tower, or the Dunston Rocket as it became known.

Owen Luder Partnership, architects, designed the new accommodation. Luder was an advocate of the 'Brutalist' postwar architecture and had designed Trinity Square, Gateshead, with the famous 'Get Carter' car park. The principal contractor was G.M. Pearson. The architects and their engineers came up with an ingenious solution to problems of the site. To prevent water flooding the site of the tower they constructed a concrete caisson or circular drum 140 feet in diameter and sunk 25 feet into the ground. The tower structure sat on this drum, whilst the hole in the centre was used for car parking. The concrete structure had facing walls of grey brick. The flats in the 29 storey building were intended for single people or couples without children, with families housed in the adjacent blocks where flats with up to four bedrooms were provided. To create a community spirit and avoid isolation a social club, supermarket and fourteen shops were included in the development. Construction began in 1968 and the first residents moved into the tower in April 1971.

Dunston Rocket (Gateshead Libraries).

The Derwent Tower was not the usual rectangular slab. It was septagonal in plan, with the core surrounded by full height fins to provide bay windows for the 196 flats within. The flats had double-glazing, gas-ducted central heating and extensive views from the upper storeys. Two 10,000 gallon water tanks were installed between floors 10 and 11. With the lower accommodation blocks clustered like supports around its base and flying buttresses rising up to the fifth floor to spread the foundations, it resembled one of the space rockets at Cape Canaveral, ready to take astronauts to the stars, and the nickname of the 'Dunston Rocket' stuck in the public imagination.

As the Council anticipated, the tower became a landmark on Tyneside, but maintenance problems, particularly with the lifts, and trying to maintain and clean such a high building, were expensive. The underground carpark flooded on several occasions. The Rocket was not upgraded as other less elaborate tower blocks were, and in 2007 Gateshead Council moved the remaining occupants to less airy accommodation. It was decided to demolish the tower as part of another redevelopment of the Ravensworth Road area. The Rocket was demolished from the top storey down from January to September 2012 and Clavering Court, a new housing for over 55s, was constructed. Nothing remains of this unique and innovative example of Council housing.

Right: The Rocket and the terraces it was intended to replace in 2008 (Richard Pears).

Whickham Workers' Educational Association
by Lillian Unsworth

Founded in 1903, by Alfred and Frances Mansbridge, members of the Cooperative movement, the WEA is a charity and UK's largest voluntary provider of adult education, delivering 9,500 part time courses for over 74,000 people each year in England and Scotland. With the WEA learning is friendly, accessible and on your doorstep. In the North East, classes ranging from Painting and Drawing, Art Appreciation, foreign languages, to history, are available in branches across the North East.

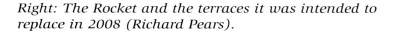

One of the most famous WEA groups was the Ashington Art Appreciation class, better known as the Pitmen Painters. They first met on 29th October 1934 in the Ashington YMCA hall. All of the members were miners and their lecturer was Dr Robert Lyon, Master of Painting and Lecturer in Fine Art at Armstrong College, Durham University. The work of the Pitmen Painters became widely admired and exhibited in art galleries throughout the British Isles. A collection of their paintings is displayed at Woodhorn Colliery Museum, Northumberland.

In the early 1960s, the Whickham Branch of the WEA was launched. It was very successful, led by such local well-known people including Alan Oates, Pat and Pete Lawther, Ralph Dunton, Geoff Linley and Alan Vanner to name but a few. In 1961, led by their tutor Helen Bowling, they published 'Some Chapters in the History of Whickham'. At the present time, Whickham branch provides classes in Art Appreciation, History and Crime Scene Investigation. We have a very loyal group of members and would welcome newcomers who may wish to join our classes in the Whickham Community Centre.

Left: The WEA publication 'Some Chapters in the History of Whickham'.

A Living Memorial to a Gallipoli Casualty
John Oswald Detchon of the Royal Naval Division
by Richard Pears

The catastrophe of the First World War brought tragedy to families across the country. One family in Whickham, sought to create a living memorial to their lost son in the form of an oak tree. This tree can be seen at 49 Cornmoor Road, Whickham and commemorates John Oswald Detchon of the Royal Naval Division, killed in action at Gallipoli. Mr John Mitchell of Whickham brought the existence of this tree to the attention of Whickham Local History Society, concerned that some future owner might cut down the tree. The following article is intended to prevent this and perpetuate the name of John Oswald Detchon in his home town.

The Royal Naval Division was raised by the First Lord of the Admiralty, Winston Churchill, in August 1914 from Royal Navy, Royal Marines and Royal Naval Volunteer Reserve personnel. They retained naval ranks but exchanged their bluejackets for khaki when deployed to the Continent. The Division was formed into battalions: Hood, Hawke, Drake, Benbow, Collingwood, Howe, Nelson and Anson Battalions, and the Royal Marine Brigade. The Division fought throughout the Western Front and at Gallipoli in Turkey. The British, French, Australian and New Zealand invasion of Gallipoli was intended to seize control of the Dardenelles peninsula, keep Turkey out of the war, and open the sea route to supply their ally Russia through the

The Gallipoli Oak Tree on Cornmoor Road.

Mediterranean Sea and Black Sea. However, the plans for the attack were not kept secret, allowing the Turks and their German allies to prepare defences before the Allies landed. Of the 75,000 Allied troops allocated for the Dardanelles landings in April 1915, some 10,000 were drawn from the Royal Naval Division. On 6th May the Anson, Howe and Hood Battalions, fighting alongside the Lancashire Fusiliers, penetrated the Turkish lines for a third of a mile, capturing the forward and second line trenches, the most substantial advance recorded in the campaign. There they stayed, exposed to Turkish artillery and snipers, until the hard-won territory was given up. By the end of July 1915, the Royal Naval Division had lost over 2,000 officers and men. By the time the Allies evacuated the Gallipoli peninsula in January 1916, some 46,000 Allied soldiers were dead and 220,000 injured. Among those who did not return was John Oswald Detchon from Whickham.

John Oswald Detchon, aged 19, an Able Seaman in the Hood Battalion of the Royal Naval Division, died of wounds on 8th May 1915. His death was reported on page 3 of 'The Times' of 24th May 1915. His service number was RY/323. He was the son of George and Margaret (née Crone) Detchon, of Hope Cottage, Cornmoor Road, Whickham. As with all Royal Navy personnel killed in action his name is recorded on a memorial at his home base, in this instance the Chatham Naval Memorial, as well as on the War Memorial on the village green in Whickham. John's family, with their loved one lying far from home, provided a very personal memorial for their lost son and brother. At the end of their garden, hard by the public footpath, they planted an acorn. That acorn has now grown into a substantial oak tree. John Oswald Detchon's 'Heart of Oak' flourishes today in the village he loved.

John Oswald Detchon commemorated on Whickham War Memorial.